There are many things you can do to say *I love you.*

♥ ♥ ♥

After you use his car, fill the tank with gasoline.

Send a plant to his office thanking him for last night.

Flirt with him at a party when you know you look beautiful. A wink over everybody else's head says, "You are best of all."

Give him a shampoo and blow-dry his hair.

Offer to go fishing with him if he cannot find a buddy.

Picture in your mind all the other women who would love to have him, and remind yourself that he *chose you. It will make you realize how lucky you are.*

400 CREATIVE WAYS TO SAY I LOVE YOU

BY ALICE CHAPIN

LIVING BOOKS
Tyndale House Publishers, Inc.
Wheaton, Illinois

Cover photo by Robert Cushman Hayes

Interior illustrations by Gregory Reinhart

Sixth printing, April 1987

Library of Congress Catalog Card Number 84-51764
ISBN 0-8423-0919-5, paper
Copyright 1981 by Alice Chapin
Printed in the United States of America

I love you, *Norman*.

CONTENTS

HOW TO LOVE YOUR MAN CREATIVELY

If I had the gift of being able to speak in other languages without learning them, and could speak in every language there is in all of heaven and earth, but didn't love others, I would only be making noise. If I had the gift of prophecy and knew all about what is going to happen in the future, knew everything about *everything*, but didn't love others, what good would it do? Even if I had the gift of faith so that I could speak to a mountain and make it move, I would still be worth nothing at all without love. If I gave everything I have to poor people, and if I were burned alive for preaching the Gospel but didn't love others, it would be of no value whatever.

Love is very patient and kind, never jealous or envious, never boastful or proud, never haughty or selfish or rude. Love does not demand its own way. It is not irritable or touchy. It does not hold grudges and will hardly even notice when others do it wrong. It is never glad about injustice, but rejoices whenever truth wins out. If you love someone, you will be loyal to him no matter what the cost. You will always believe in him, always expect the best of him, and always stand your ground in defending him.

1 Corinthians 13:1-7 *(The Living Bible)*

Dear Wives:

In Atlanta, near my home, is a bookstore run by a very wise woman. She often posts provocative messages on her outdoor advertising board. One of them was, *The best thing a woman can do for her children is to love their father.*

I had been particularly sensitive to my lack of an outward show of affection toward my good husband whom I love deeply. Every time I read the sobering truths in the Bible's great love chapter (1 Corinthians 13), I always wanted to do a better job of showing that I care. But how do you begin to put new love into an old marriage? How do you suddenly start to make apparent all the tenderness, respect, and admiration you feel?

In the past four years, I have read aloud the same passage in Corinthians to hundreds of women in my Christian-oriented marriage enrichment classes and asked them to question themselves as to whether they are loving their man that completely. Almost universally, they agreed that we talk that kind of love but do not live it, especially in our own homes. Many expressed a desire to begin more actively to show their hidden feelings of devotion; but like me, they lacked original ideas. However, each shared a few outstanding gestures of affection through a survey I passed out, and after a while I had collected hundreds, which I began to share with other students.

Everyday goodwill overtures involve imagination, knowing a lot about the other person, and sometimes, sheer willpower. They are the sugar and spice that help keep the relationship pleasant, memorable, and permanent. It is the wife who knows best what causes her husband to laugh, be satisfied, content, or pleased. She can tailor her love-in-action exactly, and if she is not very imaginative, she can blatantly copy workable ideas from other women, always being sensitive, of course, to her husband's unique personality and special needs. That is the purpose of this book. It is a collection of practical, copyable ways that the world's most knowledgeable marriage experts—wives themselves—have given love away to the men in their lives.

One wife, married nineteen years, said, "Like almost everyone else, I had been demanding of him, 'Make me happy!' Last year, when I purposely began to show my deep feelings with small, special favors, I became more fulfilled myself and the big surprise bonus came when I found him looking for ways to please me. I had forgotten that love breeds love and establishes a cycle, often giving magnificent overflow back to the giver. Jesus was really smart! He knew the ripple effect of love when he summed up marching orders for his followers by telling them to 'Love your neighbor as yourself.' It seems the whole world is running after love and trying to get it by demanding, instead of giving more of themselves away."

A Kentucky wife shared, "The creativity and fun involved in the 'how' of pleasing someone else in extraordinary ways removed boredom from my marriage and added excitement. There is real satisfaction in ministering and yielding to a person you dearly care about, especially if you have made up your mind to do it for no other reason than that you want to."

Which part of marriage will your husband and you remember in ten or twenty years? Will it be the harping, the boredom, or the happy, tender memories you purposely planned? However, will he know how much you care if you do not show him? Small, friendly deeds say, "You are on my mind," and add mellow feelings that bond a couple together. Better loving has to start somewhere. Why not with you?

Each idea in this book is a little outward statement of affection made by some wife to her man.

Feel free to borrow a few that fit your personality and your husband's personality and start to elevate your love level.

Alice Chapin
Newnan, Georgia

P.S. I have purposely changed names and places to avoid embarrassing any of those who contributed so freely to this book.

HOW TO LOVE
YOUR MAN
CREATIVELY

THINGS YOU DO
1

When I showed this chapter to a friend, married nine years, her comment was, "But I thought a wife could settle in and stop all that nonsense after the first year of marriage." No wonder her husband complains of being taken for granted!

Loving works have to be included in daily life along with loving words. Tender feelings die when daily courtesies, special kindnesses, and touchings fall by the wayside and there are only words left to display love. The smart wife will be on the lookout for little things to add rare joy to her husband's day. Miniscule loving actions performed on days when you're really not in the mood are powerful messengers that say clearly, "I am willing to bother because you are worth it." There are a myriad of things to do that say *I love you:*

♥ ♥ ♥

Kiss him hello at the door.

Teach the kids to hug Daddy when he comes into the house after work at night.

♥ ♥ ♥

Stick a sign up inside the kitchen cupboard door: *If my marriage is going to succeed, I need to be a good forgiver.*

♥ ♥ ♥

Send a plant to his office thanking him for last night.

♥ ♥ ♥

Picture in your mind all the other women who would love to have him, and remind yourself that *he* chose *you*. It will make you realize how lucky you are.

♥ ♥ ♥

After you use his car, fill the tank with gasoline.

♥ ♥ ♥

When he goes off to work, walk with him to the car once in a while. (Six military wives, all living in a row of duplexes, were stimulated by a chapel seminar to try this. What fun they had one morning when every one of them was in a driveway at the same time seeing their spouses off to a 7:30 A.M. office call!)

Send a plant to his office thanking him for last night.

Cut expenses. Balance the checkbook as soon as the monthly statement arrives.

♥ ♥ ♥

If you manage the budget, determine to set aside pocket money, plus some extra for his hobbies. Manage the money with thoughts of how he would have it done.

♥ ♥ ♥

Say to yourself, "Recreation and fun are just as important as paying the electric bill." Budget money regularly for such things as the circus, a concert, a weekend at the ocean, miniature golf, skating, square dancing, gasoline for a drive in the country, etc.

♥ ♥ ♥

Sometimes let him decide which movie or concert to go to. Go anyway, whether you like it or not.

♥ ♥ ♥

Pray for him. If you are not doing it, then who is? Pray for his success in business, for inner peace despite responsibilities, and for his health. Pray for his relationship with you, the kids, his parents, and boss. You can pray these Scripture verses for him: Philippians 1:9-11.

Flirt with him at a party when you know you look beautiful. A wink over everybody else's head says, "You are best of all."

♥ ♥ ♥

Call him at work once in a while and tell him you are thinking about him.

♥ ♥ ♥

Fight the urge to call him ten times a day and win.

♥ ♥ ♥

Surprise him (only occasionally) by stopping by his place of work to tell him some news he will enjoy hearing.

♥ ♥ ♥

Consider your marriage as a sacrament. Keep in mind that God was listening when you made your vows. (A Georgia woman says, "I feel strongly that telling my husband I had no escape hatches in my mind about marriage is the thing that has kept us trying to work out our problems. After I told him that leaving is never an option with me, he never again threatened to get out during a bad argument. My friend Julia, trying to force her husband's hand, told him she would leave if he did not change. Her quickly spoken promise, sadly, had to be lived out to protect her pride, even though she really wanted to stay.")

Give him a record such as Olivia Newton-John's "I Honestly Love You." Tell him that is how you feel about him.

♥ ♥ ♥

Keep his picture in your wallet, on the dresser, or on your desk at work.

♥ ♥ ♥

Carry a lock of his hair in your wallet.

♥ ♥ ♥

When you are on a trip together, offer to drive the last hour or two.

♥ ♥ ♥

When he tells a joke, determine not to help him nor give away the punch line.

♥ ♥ ♥

In trouble? Sick? Need refreshing? Read Psalm 57:16 together and say with the writer, "In the shadow of thy wings will I make my refuge until these calamities be overpast." Others are:

Psalm 121:3-8
Hebrews 13:5b, 6
Ephesians 3:20
2 Chronicles 16:9a

Smell good when he comes home from work.

♥ ♥ ♥

Buy or make a card or nutty little gift for no
special reason. Wrap it up and give it to him
lovingly. Be sure it matches his hobbies or in-
terests . . . perhaps a cassette tape of his favorite
recording artist, a new set of barbecue tools, a
package of new variety seeds, a red cotton hand-
kerchief, a half dozen sticky buns, or a pair of
shorts with hearts. (One woman gift-wrapped a
package of Tootsie Rolls because her husband is
the only one in the house who likes them.)

♥ ♥ ♥

When he is comfortable in his easy chair and the
TV programs change, ask, "What would you like to
watch now?" Change the channel for him.

♥ ♥ ♥

Take returns back to the store for him. Most men
feel humiliated by this job.

♥ ♥ ♥

Give him a shampoo and blow-dry his hair.

♥ ♥ ♥

When he is tired, answer the phone for him. Take
name and number so he can call back later.

Learn to say no firmly to too many social invitations that seem to be interfering with good temperaments and family life, especially during holiday seasons.

♥ ♥ ♥

Order fireplace wood and buy a new record. Send him an invitation for a "just me and you picnic" in front of the fire on your new fur rug. (To insure privacy, one woman sent her teen sons to a friend's house for one night with piles of comic books and snacks.)

♥ ♥ ♥

Offer to go fishing with him if he cannot find a buddy.

♥ ♥ ♥

Suggest a camping trip or something else he likes to do, even though these are not your favorite things.

♥ ♥ ♥

If you hate having him go off for a weekend with the boys, purposely show your goodwill anyway by getting up to serve a sausage and pancake breakfast in your best hairdo and makeup at 3:30 A.M. Or, get up looking pretty to see him off. (Tennesseean Mary T. says, "I found out it feels good to say, 'Have fun!' and I loved the big, broad smile he gave me.")

Be patient when he dawdles at the automotive counter when you are shopping together.

♥ ♥ ♥

Volunteer occasionally to take the car to the service garage and wait for it.

♥ ♥ ♥

Ask him to have lunch with you and look beautiful for him and his coworkers when you arrive. A hairdresser's appointment just before lunch will not hurt. Afterwards suggest a motel and ask if he can get the afternoon off. Even if he cannot, he will love you for asking.

♥ ♥ ♥

Put your arms around him from the rear. Tell him he smells nice. Massage his back a little. Lick his neck and leave. Teasing is part of the fun.

♥ ♥ ♥

Keep his pants pressed. Schedule this into your plans every few days without being asked.

♥ ♥ ♥

Have a photograph taken of yourself. This is a very personal gift only you can give. Or, have family pictures put into a cube paperweight for his desk.

Run his bath water now and then.

♥ ♥ ♥

On his birthday, draw a bath for him, adding
bubbles or bath oil. Put a floating flower on top
and lay out two towels, two washcloths, and two
bars of soap. Pin a flower in your hair. Tell him
you will join him by candlelight. Or play geisha
and give him a bath with a big sponge.

♥ ♥ ♥

On his birthday, get up early, lay out his clothes,
put toothpaste on the brush, arrange conveniently
his razor, shaving lotion, comb, anything else he
uses to get off to work.

♥ ♥ ♥

On his birthday, make a badge for him saying: *I am
not getting older, but better.*

♥ ♥ ♥

Occasionally, watch a TV sports program with him
that you do not particularly enjoy. Fix snacks.

♥ ♥ ♥

Turn the TV off during meals to encourage
conversation.

Have his favorite music playing when he comes
home from work.

♥ ♥ ♥

If you work, too, agree together to reserve
weekends for each other.

♥ ♥ ♥

Buy a black nightgown.

♥ ♥ ♥

Kiss him when he is reading. Once in a while, kiss
his hands.

♥ ♥ ♥

Be sentimental and frame the greeting card he
sends you or put it obviously in a favorite book as
a bookmark.

♥ ♥ ♥

Go to the department store and do not charge
anything.

♥ ♥ ♥

When he asks, promise not to live dangerously. Do
you drive too fast? Smoke or drink too much?
Swim alone sometimes? (Nancy had wanted to
lose weight. She says, "I finally got around to it
because Jim asked that I always wear the seat belt.

I hated to do it because he always had to adjust it smaller for himself and it reminded him that I wasn't as small as I used to be. Besides protecting my life, that seat belt made me think of Weight Watchers to *safe*-guard my marriage also, and I lost thirty pounds!")

♥ ♥ ♥

Leave a note for him asking: "Can we get away Saturday, just you and me?"
Yes _____   No _____   Why not? _____
Six Flags _____   Picnic and pillows _____
The lake _____   Hiking in mountains _____
Will you meet me by the car at 7 A.M.?
Yes _____   No _____   Where? _____

♥ ♥ ♥

Send a telegram inviting him to a weekend away with you. Make all the arrangements yourself.

♥ ♥ ♥

Read Scripture together for instruction from God about the role of husband and wife in marriage:

Matthew 23:11, 12   *1 Peter 3:1-11*
Colossians 3:1-15   *Genesis 2:18-25*
Ephesians 5:21-33

Use a concordance for other Bible verses about marriage. (A pastor's wife from Atlanta philosophizes, "If we don't follow God's directions for marriage, we can expect to have to live with the consequences.")

Leave a love letter pinned to a freshly laundered shirt in the closet, inside a book he is reading, or in his lunch bag. (Careful! One husband gave his lunch to a secretary, not knowing the note was inside the bag. She chased him for a month!)

♥ ♥ ♥

Make a tape-recorded love letter for him.

♥ ♥ ♥

Eat a family meal on TV trays in the den or living room so you do not disturb his puzzle or model on the kitchen table.

♥ ♥ ♥

Buy him something sexy such as a velour robe, bikini shorts, a new book on sex; or purchase matching pajamas, swim jackets, shirts, or coffee mugs to tell the world you belong together and are proud of it.

♥ ♥ ♥

Massage his temples when he has a headache or hold him close in bed when he feels down. (A college student's wife said, "My husband was up all night working on his thesis. At 7 A.M., he ate breakfast, then fell in bed. I left the kids at the breakfast table and snuggled in bed a few minutes with him, holding him in my arms and then rubbing his back until he fell asleep. When he woke up that afternoon, he hugged me and told me how great he thought it was to have a wife who really understands.")

♥ ♥ ♥

Have the newspaper waiting by his favorite chair.

♥ ♥ ♥

Fold the newspaper after you read it so the pages are in order for him.

♥ ♥ ♥

Gather up and frame his important memory items (medals, ribbons, citations, honor and graduation certificates, newspaper clippings, etc.). Display them on the living room or den wall. He will know you are proud of him.

♥ ♥ ♥

If he remarks that his hair is getting thin, remind him that no one likes fat hair anyway.

♥ ♥ ♥

Once in a while, wake him gently with a kiss.

♥ ♥ ♥

Attempt to be cheerful even though you do not feel that way.

Try to use the word "ours" instead of "mine"
whenever you can.

♥ ♥ ♥

Tell him your wedding band means a lot to you.
Share some pleasant thoughts you have when you
look at it, and tell him you never want to remove
it. Then never do.

♥ ♥ ♥

Learn as much as you can about his work.

♥ ♥ ♥

Agree on a place you would like to travel together.
Begin to collect brochures and books describing
it. Put a bank on the dresser to save for the trip.

♥ ♥ ♥

Togetherness counts. Study Sunday school lessons
together. Leave the dishes and take a bike ride
together. Build a snowman together. Wash the car
or peel tomatoes for canning. (An Alabama wife
shares with a smile, "We giggled for weeks about
the Christmas plum pudding we made together
because when I left the room, he cracked the eggs
open with a screwdriver!")

♥ ♥ ♥

Privacy counts, too. Allow breathing room for
separate hobbies, friends, and times alone. Pushing

too hard for togetherness can be just as hard on a couple as too little time together.

♥ ♥ ♥

Never ask him to do anything you can do for yourself.

♥ ♥ ♥

On Mother's Day, send him a telegram saying: "Thank you for making me the mother of our beautiful children."

♥ ♥ ♥

Keep a diary and read it over together in a few years.

♥ ♥ ♥

Never throw away his favorite old clothes or furniture, no matter how tacky they look to you. ("Three years ago, Ed angrily grabbed the raggedy, stained workshirt I had been using to drape the bird cage, saying no bird was going to sleep later than he. He meant it. Ed still wears the shirt to work on the car!" says an Ohio wife.)

♥ ♥ ♥

Never compare him with old boyfriends, your father, or former husband.

Put flowers he brings you on the table for supper even if the color clashes with the tablecloth. Dry one bouquet or frame a special flower.

♥ ♥ ♥

Make a pot of coffee or pop popcorn for him when he gets home from a lengthy meeting at 1 A.M. Or, just for fun, try saying aloud in your most seductive voice, as he wearily climbs into bed beside you in the dark, "Is that you, Rock?" If neither of you can go to sleep right away, try giving him the Honest-to-Goodness, Very, Very Official Decor Test right there with the lights out, by asking, "What color are the bed sheets tonight?"

♥ ♥ ♥

Once in a while, give him the mail first or share the feature section of the newspaper.

♥ ♥ ♥

Make the tenth (or whatever) of every month a special day because you were married that day. Eat out or have a special candlelight dinner at home with flowers on the table.

♥ ♥ ♥

Sit over next to him when he drives the car for an evening out. This will take a little courage if you have not done this for a while. Enjoy together the reaction of the kids and neighbors.

Watch him work out with weights.

♥ ♥ ♥

Touch his rear while riding behind on the
escalator.

♥ ♥ ♥

Exchange back scratchings.

♥ ♥ ♥

Once in a while when you are out with the girls,
stop by the ice cream store and bring home
the most scrumptious concoction on the menu
just for him.

♥ ♥ ♥

Sew for him. (A pair of twins, married to brothers,
made their husbands plaid slacks and velour
shirts. The men went with them to pick out the
fabric. One also made her man a robe, then
embroidered an *I love you* heart and sewed it
inside. The other made hubby a bowling towel
decorated with a bowling pin and smile face, a
head cover for a tennis racket, and a tie for a new
suit because he could not find one he liked in the
store. One twin giggles, "No more crocheting
doilies for the back of his armchair, though! The
barber pulled one off Jack's back, teasing him
about how styles have changed!")

Help him fill out job applications. Write notes for him to his business associates, and attend conferences where your husband is speaking or participating. If he brings work home, ask if you can help; or go to the office occasionally to help him catch up.

♥ ♥ ♥

Decorate his office (as a surprise?).

♥ ♥ ♥

Get sentimental together when you sell an old car or your house. (New Yorker Amy T. says, "I told my husband I really hated to see the car go because we had brought home three babies from the hospital in it and I reminisced about the out-of-this-world New Hampshire trip we took in it, camping out under the pines for two weeks. It was fun to see him get nostalgic, too, laughing about how we called it our struggle buggy because repair bills started coming in before car payments had stopped.")

♥ ♥ ♥

Feed the kids early or perhaps serve them dinner in their rooms or in front of the TV once a week so you and your man can have dinner alone and time to talk.

Get the kids to help you cook up surprises for Dad:

When he has done something to make you proud or happy, stop by the bakery for a goodie and top it with a sparkler or trick light bulb that needs no plug, available in novelty stores. (One wife planned a Thanksgiving dinner in January because her husband escaped injury in a car accident. Later, she printed MASTER SALESMAN on a blue ribbon and laid it by hubby's dinner plate when he sold a huge insurance policy. The kids loved the idea and made a HERO banner when Dad came home with the golf trophy.)

For no reason at all, celebrate Dad's Day some Saturday. He gets breakfast and the paper in bed, the lawn mowed or leaves raked, two tickets to a ball game with Mom, a gift, and his favorite supper.

Plan a guest of honor dinner for Father's Day. (In one Miami family, Mom and the four daughters dressed up in good clothes, served roast beef to the family on the best china, and each gave a testimonial of why Dad is a great guy. The wife's comment: "Ed had been working unearthly hours and there had been terrible job pressure put on him. Support of the family was just what he needed. It brought tears of gratefulness to his eyes.")

On Dad's birthday, make a special wall display of his baby pictures. He will feel honored by all the fuss and will get a kick out of seeing the kids hoot and holler over the old photos.

♥ ♥ ♥

Purposely touch, hold hands, or kiss sometimes when the kids are around. Their respect for both of you will likely go sky high, and as a bonus they probably will copy you when they get married. (A Birmingham pastor says, "Children worry about their own parents when they see friends' moms and dads divorcing. It makes kids feel secure about their home situation seeing Mother and Father show physical love for each other.")

♥ ♥ ♥

Collect the younger children and pets and be waiting outside on the front steps for Daddy to come home from work sometimes. (One wife called her husband ahead and told him she and the two boys would be waiting out front to sing a new song they had been practicing for him. She said it meant a lot to him since he had had a difficult day at work.)

♥ ♥ ♥

Support him in disciplining the kids. Stick with him and back up his decisions. Never let the kids play you against each other. If you do not agree with his discipline, let him know privately.

If you are going to interview a baby-sitter so you can take a job, let your husband go with you for the interview. He will not be so likely to resent someone else's caring for the children and will feel more comfortable about their safety.

♥ ♥ ♥

THINGS YOU SAY
(OR DO NOT SAY)
2

Ill-chosen words can injure without leaving a
visible trace, and deceitful or inappropriate ones
can turn a marvelous day into a disaster. But
honest words, carefully selected, can help your
man like himself better, save a lot of heartache,
and foster good feelings.

Here are some loving phrases to use when
applicable:

"It's wonderful to have such a handsome man
come home to me each night."

"You look outstanding today."

"You make that suit look great."

"I don't feel complete without you."

"I appreciate the way you treat my mother."

"I appreciate the way you have provided for our
family all these years."

"It is great to be married to a man who takes troubles and problems to God and seeks his will for life. It makes me feel secure."

"You come first in my life, before the kids, career, anything."

"I am glad I married you."

"You are the best friend I have."

"As long as we are together, I can lose everything and my world would still be OK."

"If you asked me to marry you today, I would."

"I wanted you today."

"I missed you today."

"I want you."

"I'll be waiting for you tonight. Don't forget to come home."

"I couldn't get you out of my mind today."

"I love the way you make love."

"It's nice to wake up next to you."

"I will always love you."

"You set off fireworks for me."

"I am proud that you are my man."

"I need you."

"I love your square chin."

"I like a man with a narrow waist and broad shoulders like yours."

"I love you for handling the kids' argument so well."

"I admire your perseverance."

"I love to see your eyes sparkle when you smile."

"Strange. We used to be the same age when we were in high school together. Today you look younger." (To be said with a friendly nudge and a peck-kiss.)

Read these for guidance in speaking:

Proverbs 21:23   *James 1:26*
Proverbs 18:13   *Philippians 2:14, 15*
Proverbs 16:23, 24   *Titus 3:2*
Matthew 12:36, 37

♥ ♥ ♥

Tell him you want to please him as a wife. Just once ask, "What can I do to make you happier?"

♥ ♥ ♥

Tell him that after you have looked around and listened to other husbands, you realize you have it really good. Perhaps you can say to him, "You are far superior to any other husband I have ever met." (A beautiful legal secretary's husband told her this meant more to him than anything she had ever said to him. He responded with a red rosebud in a vase on the kitchen shelf.)

Tell him you love him at least once a day.

♥ ♥ ♥

While admiring bigger diamond engagement rings together in a jewelry store window, say, "I would rather have mine because it means having you."

♥ ♥ ♥

When visitors come, show them the hobby projects or craft items your man has made. Tell your guests they are his special creations and how much you enjoy having them in the house. Example: "John made this beautiful table in his workshop. He painted all those lovely watercolors on that south wall, too."

♥ ♥ ♥

Tell him you understand how difficult it is to be chief supporter of the family with several people depending on him for a majority of their food, clothing, and shelter. You can say, "It is wonderful to have a man who is my lover, provider, and protector."

♥ ♥ ♥

Appreciate him! (After he had shingled her aged mother's house on four hot, sweaty Saturdays, an Akron wife told her husband, "You deserve a new suit for doing that. Let's go get one for you.")

When he asks you to do small things, such as take shirts to the laundry, sew on a button, replace a pocket, or iron handkerchiefs, get into the habit of saying "OK, I will." Willingness without grumbling is refreshing and shows you take his little needs seriously. Also, he will be a lot more likely to respond the same way when you make requests.

♥ ♥ ♥

If your husband is quiet around people, give him a chance to talk in group conversations with phrases like, "Why not tell that story about . . ." or "Jim, you tell them about that . . ." or "Jim, I will let you answer that question. . . ." This kind of approach encourages a quiet man to express himself.

♥ ♥ ♥

Things to say about Dad to the kids (from Marie, a mother of four children, including a set of triplets):

"Dad is head of our house. Let's listen when he talks."

"Fathers are to listen to, not argue with."

"Not right now, please. I am talking to your father."

"Dad works hard for us and is tired tonight. Let's try to make a quiet evening for him." (When Marie said this, the kids quickly took up the idea by playing soft music on the stereo, bringing Dad his slippers and iced tea, trimming the hedge, making the weekly phone call to Grandma for him, and promising not to squabble.)

♥ ♥ ♥

Marie gives other examples of how to brag enthusiastically about your husband to the kids:

   "Daddy is a wonderful outdoorsman. He taught me to identify nearly every bird and tree."

   "Dad handled that cranky neighbor with the mean dog really well, didn't he?"

   "Hooray for Dad! He's a volleyball champ!"

   "Good going, Jim. Not many men get a promotion after only six months."

   "Our dad has a green thumb." (Marie's family sang these words to the tune of "Happy Birthday" when Father won the local garden club award for the best lawn on the street.)

♥ ♥ ♥

If he will not go to church with you, tell him once or twice that you would like him to, then keep quiet about it.

♥ ♥ ♥

Never, never humiliate your husband by talking about him to others when he is right there in the room.

Never criticize him or apologize for him in public.

♥ ♥ ♥

Decide firmly that you will never talk about your marriage problems to anyone except God or a well-chosen counselor. The more you gripe, the more you will burn with resentment.

♥ ♥ ♥

Never, never say, "I told you so."

♥ ♥ ♥

Determine to keep secrets when he confides in you. Spilling secrets can destroy communication because he will not want to share again with a tattletale.

♥ ♥ ♥

Never talk in bitterness against your husband to your children.

♥ ♥ ♥

Refrain from making derogatory remarks about men in general, telling jokes about their roving eyes, feelings of superiority, driving ability, machismo, or whatever. Your husband would probably take such talk personally.

♥ ♥ ♥

LOVING YOUR IN-LAWS
3

Dear loving, gentle, wonderful husband Bob:

I quit.

Our in-laws are smothering us.

Love,

Janice

Janice confided to the marriage counselor that Bob's relatives would pop in unannounced, day or night, and that his jobless kid brother liked to camp out on their couch. In-laws sometimes stayed two weeks, forcing the children to give up bedrooms and exhausting everyone—especially Janice, who works full time, yet cooks all the meals. Bob's family had always opened their homes to each other and expected it from everybody.

Sometimes, relatives must be confronted about

interfering. However, uncomfortable encounters can often be avoided or made easier if a couple agrees to go out of their way with small favors to build the in-law relationship ahead of time. Smart sons and daughters will remember that it is a compliment to parents to take advantage of their wisdom and counsel whenever possible. Using them as confidantes builds good feelings.

Mary G., a level-headed Savannah wife with a feisty, sharp-tongued father-in-law, shared: "It always helps me to remember that no matter how I feel about Jerry's dad, he and his wife were God's placement to bring my excellent husband to adulthood. Somehow, despite their own bad tempers and haphazard values, they managed to instill in him the good qualities I enjoy today." A new bride whose husband's parents came from another country and culture says, "I try to look at my relatives' differences as eccentricities, not faults or weaknesses, and to allow them the freedom to be nonconformists if they want to. It adds zest to life, having a wisecracking tobacco-chewing uncle, an outlandish aunt who collects canaries, husbands, and bagel recipes, and a 250-pound mother-in-law who yells at everybody, carries placards for radical street rallies, and reads palms. It may just be that these people, however contentious or odd they seem, were placed in my life as God's finishing tool to mellow me and enhance my ability to love people."

Trying hard to love your husband's relatives demonstrates that you care for him.

Keep a birthday list of his brothers, sisters, and other family members. Make it your job to send cards to each on the appropriate date. Remember your mother-in-law and father-in-law on anniversaries also.

♥ ♥ ♥

Write often to his mother if you live far away; or call her. Most husbands want to keep in touch but have little time or inclination.

♥ ♥ ♥

Write notes to grandparents about your children. Send them cards on Mother's Day and Father's Day and be sure to include family photos when you can.

♥ ♥ ♥

On Mother's or Father's Day, send a note to his parents thanking them for providing you with such a good man. Or, compliment your husband in front of his parents and tell them, "You raised a fine son."

♥ ♥ ♥

Visit his relatives with him.

Be patient with his parents even if they are a bit trying. Love them for your husband's sake.

♥ ♥ ♥

Frame and hang pictures of him and his family. You might add those of your own folks and call it your family wall album.

♥ ♥ ♥

Send your husband a love note when he is visiting his parents.

♥ ♥ ♥

Allow him to invite his mother and father for a visit. Ask God to give you a spirit of love and thankfulness for having them in your home. Ask that resentfulness about invasion of privacy be removed.

♥ ♥ ♥

Discourage lengthy visits by relatives.

♥ ♥ ♥

Ask his mother for the recipe to make his favorite dessert.

♥ ♥ ♥

Buy a piggy bank to save quarters for the family to fly back home and visit his folks.

*Write often to his mother if you live far away;
or call her. Most husbands want to keep in touch but
have little time or inclination.*

Never tell a mother-in-law joke.

♥ ♥ ♥

Never side with your father or mother in arguments against your mate.

♥ ♥ ♥

Read Matthew 19:4-6 to get a good perspective on what God planned for married couples in regard to in-laws.

♥ ♥ ♥

Determine not to brag about your rich or smart relatives.

♥ ♥ ♥

Determine not to depend on parents (especially financially) once you are married.

♥ ♥ ♥

Determine not to criticize his relatives. Make it a point to praise them when you can.

♥ ♥ ♥

Try to have pleasant experiences with his mother. Purposely plan a shopping trip, fashion show, or some other activity together. Try inviting both your mothers over for lunch at the same time.

Frame and hang pictures of him and his family.
You might add those of your own folks and call it your
family wall album.

Do not make your mother-in-law a scapegoat and blame her for your husband's shortcomings. You will probably be a mother-in-law someday.

♥ ♥ ♥

Here are some good rules if you are somebody's mother-in-law:

Never say anything to either your son or daughter about his or her spouse that you would not say in front of the person.

When an argument starts in your married child's home, take a walk.

Take it easy on giving advice.

♥ ♥ ♥

HOW TO LOVE
YOUR MAN
CREATIVELY

AROUND THE HOUSE
4

Instead of nagging Rick about the doorbell that needed fixing, Mary Ellen hung a pie plate and huge wooden spoon beside the back door just before he got home from work. Two hours later, the doorbell was working again. When the toilet needed repair, she taped a note to the tank that said: *I played Mount St. Helens three times today.* When they moved to the country and Rick kept forgetting to bury the garbage the first month, Mary Ellen carefully placed her shiniest pan full of potato peelings, leftover oatmeal, tomato soup, orange skin, and coffee grounds on the kitchen shelf. She hand-lettered and decorated a beautiful sign that said: *Look inside for a grand view.* Rick did and roared with laughter. He seldom forgot after that.

Searching for fun ways to handle touchy matters

or everyday situations takes effort, and your husband knows it. Taking the trouble to add a little tomfoolery, a few well-planned surprises, some sensible restraint, or a new attitude to life at home tells him that you are striving for harmony even though there is the serious business of a household to be run.

Try these:

Whistle and sing when you feel happy. Try to enjoy being right where you are. Your husband wants you satisfied in your job as his wife.

♥ ♥ ♥

Post this on the cupboard door: *To be content with what we possess is the greatest and most secure of riches.* (Cicero)

♥ ♥ ♥

Keep the house picked up. Dishes in the sink day after day, unmade beds, and things strewn all over tell him you are not keeping up your end of things, and he is disappointed. If you need help, ask for it forthrightly in a matter-of-fact voice without complaining.

♥ ♥ ♥

Do not assume all men are handy with tools. Do not expect him to do fix-it jobs just because your father could. Maybe his father never taught him how.

If several chores need doing, presenting one a day makes you look like a persistent nag. Instead, collect them into a list and tack it up once a month or so over his desk or on the bathroom door. If he forgets, make a bigger new list on brighter colored paper and post it in a more obvious place.

♥ ♥ ♥

If you have a job outside the home and he is willing to help with housework, keep in mind ways to share the work load; don't load your husband up. Feelings of being misused breed resentment.

♥ ♥ ♥

Make up your mind that if he volunteers to do a portion of the household chores, you will not criticize the way he does them.

♥ ♥ ♥

If you find your mood faltering and your attitude a problem because of too many demands on your life, schedule a "stay at home and do what you want" day (or week). Leave all the work except absolute necessities. Relax and get caught up on personal things you have been longing to do. A working wife may have to use her vacation and enlist the family's cooperation. (One husband, confronted with the idea, set aside a week of his vacation time to help out. He declared it Mother's week at home, taking the kids to Daily Vacation Bible School mornings and to the pool afternoons. Two nights, a baby-sitter was hired for Mom and Dad's night out. Mom used the days for sun-bathing, reading, sewing, and puttering. "The best vacation I ever had," she declares. "No packing, unpacking, or boring road trips with kids arguing in the back seat.")

♥ ♥ ♥

Determine never again to refer to yourself as "just a housewife." Remind yourself that child care and being a loving wife are complicated and demand-ing jobs, and that running a household is a chal-lenging career.

♥ ♥ ♥

Appreciating yourself and liking yourself makes you a better, more sensitive wife who is able to love others more. On a day when you begin feeling that your job as homemaker is unimpor-tant, try listing, as one wife-mother did, your major accomplishments; then envision the effect they may have on each member of the family one by one. (A working wife can add eight hours of paid employment outside the home.)

a. Beautiful chocolate cupcakes baked for the third grade party
b. Neat piles of sweet-smelling laundry washed, folded, and put away

c. A shiny kitchen floor
d. Child's ballet costume completed
e. Two children's toys, husband's favorite shirt, and aged mother's dress repaired
f. The aroma of baked chicken as my family comes in the door
g. A content, clean baby
h. A predictable, good-natured mother and wife in the evening
i. Sunday school lesson prepared
j. Seven quarts of sweet chunk pickles canned, the family's favorite

Little things can be such big acts of love. If he likes chocolate pie and you have time to make it, serve it once a week. If he is crazy about corned beef and cabbage, cook it even if you dislike the odor. If he likes his shirt collars pressed down, do it. If he thinks the jackets should be removed from all new books, strip them. If messy butter dishes are his pet peeve, use a clean one daily.

Develop an "I'll help you, you help me" attitude. (Says Nell, a New York housewife and mother of five daughters, "Doing dishes, bagging yard debris, or picking green beans together for supper deepens our friendship and appreciation of each other. When I grabbed a sponge and pail and went at the muddy car right alongside my husband, he sat down and helped me shell peas on the front porch that evening because he knows how tedious the task is and how I detest the job.")

♥ ♥ ♥

If you have kids, wipe out the bathroom sink a couple of times a day, and especially on weekends when the whole family is home.

♥ ♥ ♥

Respect his privacy when he goes into the bathroom, bedroom, or garage and shuts the door. Do not ask questions or barge in. If there is an emergency, knock first before entering.

♥ ♥ ♥

Never open his mail.

♥ ♥ ♥

Leave his razors and tools alone.

♥ ♥ ♥

Take the garbage out some days without reminding him that he forgot. Never mention it again.

♥ ♥ ♥

Notice the nice things he does around the house. Purposely mention the neatly raked yard, the clean car, the repaired lawn chair.

Surprise him by doing a job he has put off, such as weeding, resubscribing to a favorite magazine, cutting the grass, polishing shoes, etc. (One wife said she washed and waxed her husband's motor-cycle!)

♥ ♥ ♥

Get up when he does in the morning. Try to look pretty and cheerful. Comb your hair and wear a decent robe. (Says a wife of five years, "I ask myself if the secretaries he will see in the office all day look better than his last glimpse of me in the morning.")

♥ ♥ ♥

Before leaving the house, tell him where you are going and when you expect to return. If he is not home, put a note on the kitchen table. Just for fun, you can sign it with a lipstick print.

♥ ♥ ♥

Ask yourself: If I were going to choose someone to live with, would I choose me? Why?

♥ ♥ ♥

Live every day with your man as if it were the last. Ask yourself: If I knew he or I were going to die tomorrow, how would I treat him today?

When possible, invite women friends in only when he is not around.

♥ ♥ ♥

Talk to girl friends on the phone when he is out of the house. Let them know you do not particularly like to chat with them in the evening when your husband is home.

♥ ♥ ♥

Take girl friends shopping only when he is not along.

♥ ♥ ♥

Here are special kitchen kindnesses some Atlanta wives shared:

Bake a birthday cake for him and take it to the office to share with his associates. Have the family join in if they can.

♥ ♥ ♥

Bake a special dessert for him to show off and share at work. (A pilot's wife says she makes her husband's favorite dessert to take on the plane with him.)

♥ ♥ ♥

Fix his favorite dish for supper some night even though no one else likes it. Tell the kids it is Dad's night and arrange materials so they can prepare build-yourself Dagwood sandwiches.

Cook collards on the day he brings them fresh from the garden, even though you are having pizza for supper. Cook the vegetables from his backyard garden even though some are pretty small.

♥ ♥ ♥

Learn to clean and cook fish, and to freeze deer meat and other bounty he brings home from outdoor trips.

♥ ♥ ♥

Peel and separate oranges; pick grapes off the stem for a bag lunch; put sugar in his coffee, butter on crackers, and sour cream on baked potato. (A doctor's wife says, "These seem like small things, but my husband appreciates me for the little favors that seem crazy or even solicitous to somebody else.")

♥ ♥ ♥

Cook pudding from scratch for him instead of making it from a box.

♥ ♥ ♥

Make his favorite lemon pie even though you are on a diet.

♥ ♥ ♥

Spend time planning in order to make meals interesting for him when he is on a special diet.

Decorate an anniversary cake with the message, "I'm glad I married you."

♥ ♥ ♥

Have the smell of fresh-baked bread in the air when your husband gets home from work.

♥ ♥ ♥

Bring iced tea or lemonade out in the yard when he is mowing the lawn on a hot day.

♥ ♥ ♥

To celebrate a very special occasion, get out your big stainless-steel round gravy bowls or good china serving bowls and fill them brimful of strawberry shortcake and whipped cream instead of serving supper.

♥ ♥ ♥

Most men like their wives with the family on holidays such as Thanksgiving and Christmas, instead of in the kitchen. Prepare food as much as possible the day before. Fix dressing, vegetables, dessert, and even set the table ahead.

♥ ♥ ♥

Turn on the stereo and light a candle for the dinner table after the kids have finished and gone out to play. Linger for good conversation.

♥ ♥ ♥

Learn to clean and cook fish, and to freeze deer meat and other bounty he brings home from outdoor trips.

HOW TO LOVE
YOUR MAN
CREATIVELY

BEDROOM LIFE
5

Good sex allows physical communication of love.
Your husband dreams about exciting sex
experiences. So do you. Marriage is meant to be
fun, and sex is half the fun. Sometimes, sensational
sex comes because one or both of the partners is
innovative and perhaps a little daring. If you are a
blusher, get over it. It is not wrong to be enticing
to your own husband. You belong to each other.
Want to burn incense in the bedroom? Try it! Buy
that sexy, fur-trimmed lounging outfit for yourself
and gold lamé shorts for him from the Frederick's
of Hollywood catalog and have a candlelight
dinner of french bread, hard sausage, and wine on
the back patio table after the kids are asleep. Why
not? Want to spread the sleeping bags out in the
backyard under the stars some night when Junior
is spending the night with Grandma? Suggest it.
Whatever pleases both of you is totally right.

Trying new things not only adds fun, it builds memories. A man or woman is not likely to go "shopping" outside if sex life is great at home.

Caution: Whatever goes on behind your bedroom door is between you and your mate forever. Describing husband-wife intimacies to a friend robs the two of you of a delicious privacy and takes away some of the magic. Sensuous secrets are made for two, and blabbing can cause deep resentment.

If you are running out of ideas to add pizazz to your bedroom life:

Place a carnation or some other flower on his pillow. Give it a special meaning so he knows what is ahead each time he sees it. A lighted candle on the dresser at 8 P.M. can also convey a secret message.

♥ ♥ ♥

Attend Marriage Encounter or one of several other marriage enrichment weekends planned for couples by various churches or religious groups. You will come home appreciating and wanting each other more. (One man's comment was, "At the marriage seminar, each couple was expected to spend time alone talking, and for the first time I was able to express to my wife my heartache about being sterile, and how I had cried myself to sleep night after night because she would never be able to carry our child. Suddenly, I was not alone in my misery, and the burden lifted.")

If you are losing weight, tell him you are doing it for him so he will have a new "you" to make love to. When the day arrives, plan something special for the bedroom.

♥ ♥ ♥

Go to bed when he does.

♥ ♥ ♥

Bathe daily.

♥ ♥ ♥

Read a good sex book together before bed occasionally.

♥ ♥ ♥

Make love in new places. Just bought a new plush carpet? Do you have a screened-in back porch? What about the living room sofa? Be creative.

♥ ♥ ♥

When you need to, wear strategic makeup to bed.

♥ ♥ ♥

Once in a while, love him awake in the early morning in your own special way.

♥ ♥ ♥

When the alarm rings in the morning, turn it off, put your arms around him, and say, "I love you."

Occasionally, cover him back up when you get out of bed in the morning. Tell him he has ten more minutes to sleep and that you will wake him then. This may mean you'll need to get up earlier.

♥ ♥ ♥

Tell him you are glad he is there when you reach out for him in the middle of the night.

♥ ♥ ♥

Suggest that next time you travel together, you find a motel with a waterbed.

♥ ♥ ♥

Rent a remote cottage where you can swim together in the nude at midnight.

♥ ♥ ♥

If you can, go back to your honeymoon hotel. Plan together and talk about how it will be to make love away from telephones, children, and other interruptions.

♥ ♥ ♥

If you cannot get away, plan a one night mini-honeymoon at home. Farm the kids out. Get a new peignoir. Serve a candlelight dinner. Have the bed covers turned back. Plan at least ten different details to make a romantic night.

If you can, go back to your honeymoon hotel. Plan together and talk about how it will be to make love away from telephones, kids, and other interruptions.

Tell your husband that the bedroom is the most important room in the house to you. Use special care and imagination to decorate it.

♥ ♥ ♥

At bedtime, shower together using a tube of liquid body shampoo. Soap him all over with your hands and let him do the same for you.

♥ ♥ ♥

Make a couple of rabbit fur toss pillows for your bed.

♥ ♥ ♥

Once in a while, spray the sheets with perfume.

♥ ♥ ♥

Buy a small electric coffee pot for the bedroom.

♥ ♥ ♥

Ask him to put a lock on the bedroom door. Tell him why.

♥ ♥ ♥

Suggest building a private balcony off your bedroom.

♥ ♥ ♥

Buy satin sheets to use now and then. (Their slipperiness makes them impractical for every day.)

*At bedtime, shower together using a tube of liquid
body shampoo. Soap him all over with your hands
and let him do the same for you.*

Bring a record player into the bedroom for quiet music.

♥ ♥ ♥

Buy and trim a little Christmas tree for the bedroom. Flashing bulbs give a special effect.

♥ ♥ ♥

Take the phone off the hook some evening when you want a private time together. Tell him what you have done.

♥ ♥ ♥

Buy a blue light bulb for the bedroom lamp.

♥ ♥ ♥

Remind yourself that men usually need sex more often than women.

♥ ♥ ♥

Purposely think thoughts about your husband that will make you a more willing bed partner.

♥ ♥ ♥

Tell him what you enjoy in lovemaking. Let him know exactly what pleases you. Show him where and how you like to be touched. How else will he know if you do not tell him? Ask what you can do to make loving better for him.

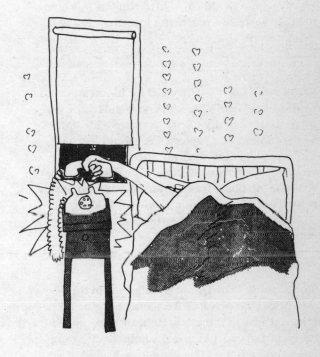

Take the phone off the hook some evening when you want a private time together. Tell him what you have done.

Tell your husband you would like to be his lover. Ask what attributes a lover should have.

♥ ♥ ♥

Carry the glow over to the next day by calling him or writing a note. You can say, "I love you" or "You are my whole world" or "I love you this morning too" or "We have a pretty hot love affair going at 29 Elm Street, don't we?"

♥ ♥ ♥

Recall often that God planned for his creatures to be thoroughly delighted, excited, and happy with their mates sexually. (Read Hebrews 13:4 and Song of Solomon, chapters 4-8.) Your husband wants you to enjoy sex, too. Specifically plan to yield to your sensual feelings in real wanton abandon, no holds barred, during intercourse. Say to yourself, "It may be an offense to God if I stubbornly refuse to enjoy the good gift of sex with my husband."

♥ ♥ ♥

Stop to think, "Lord, how wonderful!" in the middle of your private love scene. Imagine there is no one else in the world right then except your husband and you. (This really helped one young wife who said, "I was brought up ashamed of sex. My parents even felt it was wrong to see kittens born. I developed a pattern of playing hard to get and pretending I did not enjoy sex. Now, after eight months of therapy, I am able to accept the fact that sexual intercourse is God's original idea and that he made my body just right for it and wants me to be overjoyed with my husband.")

♥ ♥ ♥

Once in a while, rub his back and listen to good music in bed. Fall asleep together while listening, with no sex demands.

♥ ♥ ♥

If you find yourself running off at the mouth continually right after you get in bed together, suspect yourself of trying to avoid sex. A monologue about Junior's last report card, the broken washing machine, or your frustration with the new boss at the office is not very conducive to loving.

♥ ♥ ♥

Be awake and beautiful when he comes home from a night meeting.

♥ ♥ ♥

After good loving, say to him (if you feel this way):

"I would walk around the world for the feeling I have right now."

"I like being your lover."

"No one else could make me feel like this."

Remind yourself that there is an advantage to making love in the daytime—daylight.

♥ ♥ ♥

Start laying the groundwork for a good night life with a sensuous good morning kiss. Anticipation can brighten the whole day (and the night).

♥ ♥ ♥

Try these for fun:

Body painting with finger paints, then showering together.
A rubdown, back and front.
Make love in front of a mirror.
Sleep nude.
Remind yourselves that an active sex session can burn up 700 calories!

♥ ♥ ♥

When one of you is too tired for sex, suggest setting the alarm for 5 A.M. Early morning loving can be warm and satisfying with the house quiet and the relaxation that comes after a good night's sleep. Or, say to him, "Let's make tomorrow night special, instead. We can get the kids to bed early and have a nice supper alone, then have sex twice as good as it would be tonight." Start off the next day with a reminder of what you have in mind for the evening.

June's idea for a dark, rainy Saturday when the kids were away at camp: "We both were restless and sick of reading. Still the rain kept pounding on the roof so we couldn't get outdoors. I left a note on Gary's pillow saying, 'I am bored. Can you think of anything we could do here?' A while later when I returned, his note said, 'I sure can. Meet me here at 2 P.M.' The covers were already pulled back when I arrived."

♥ ♥ ♥

BEING BEAUTIFUL
INSIDE AND OUT

6

Your husband chose you out of all the other
terrific women in the world. What an ego booster!
Why did he do it? What beautiful things did he see
in you that he loved? Perhaps it was a size ten
figure, long, silky blonde hair, a soft-spoken
personality, spirited conversation, or your choice
of feminine clothes worn with high heels. A wise
woman will work hard to keep things intact.

Some physical beauty will slip away with the
years even though most women yearn for a
beautiful face and figure forever. The best any of
us can do is take care of our outer selves with the
help of appropriate cosmetics and the services of
a local beauty boutique, drawing consolation
from the fact that God allows husbands to grow
older along with wives.

Inner beauty is another matter. Not only can it

be truly fadeless, but it can grow daily; and because the face reflects what goes on inside, radiance can actually increase with age. There is real hope in that! Cultivating a peaceful, quiet spirit inside can transform the outer self, making eyes sparkle and smiles flow easily. Everyone admires a person with a beautiful inner disposition who quietly trusts God through all situations, sees the good in others, always wants the best for them, and desires to follow Jesus' directions to love your neighbor as yourself.

A wife can forthrightly question her husband about what he likes best and least in her after several years of marriage, and with a "chin up" attitude to avoid being hurt, map out plans to improve inside and out to please him. A youngish grandmother, age forty and married nineteen years, asked her spouse to fill out the following marital survey she created herself, telling him, "I simply want to find out some things so I can get better and better for you."

1. How can I please you more as a wife?
2. What bothers you most about our relationship right now?
3. What is the best thing about our life together right now?
4. Are there areas of our life together about which you think it is hard to communicate? What are they? How can we improve?
5. Name two minor changes you would like to see in me.

6. Name two major changes you would like to see in me in the next five years.

Months later, her husband surprised her with his own survey to determine how she would like to see him change. She admitted her disappointment with their communication, and out of that grew their decision to read together daily from *The Friendship Factor* by Alan Loy McGinnis (Augsburg Publishers) and *The Trauma of Transparency* by J. Grant Howard (Multnomah Press), both books geared to improve communication.

♥ ♥ ♥

Helps and Hints to Improve Inner Beauty

Books rated highest as attitude adjusters:

The Greatest Thing in the World by Henry Drummond (Fleming H. Revell)
The Christian's Secret of a Happy Life by Hannah Whitehall Smith (Fleming H. Revell)
The Power of Positive Thinking by Norman Vincent Peale (Prentice Hall)
What Happens When Women Pray by Evelyn Christenson (Victor Books)
Believing God for the Impossible by Bill Bright (Here's Life Publishers)
Your God Is Too Small by J. B. Phillips (Macmillan)

Prayer and Bible reading are God's beauty treatment for the inner self. Below are some specific Bible prescriptions, favorites of several pastors' wives, to match moods or problems, help unload bad feelings, and make living easier right where you are. For others, see *Let The Living Bible Help You* by Alice Chapin (Harper and Row).

If you feel:

Afraid
Romans 8:31
Isaiah 41:10, 13

Sad
Psalm 34:17-19
Habakkuk 3:17-19

Discouraged
Isaiah 43:2, 3
2 Corinthians 1:3-5

Lonesome
Romans 8:35-39
Psalm 91:1, 2

Quarrelsome
Proverbs 19:13
Proverbs 21:9, 19
Proverbs 27:15

Anxious, Worried
Matthew 6:25-34
Philippians 4:4-6
1 Peter 5:7, 10, 11
1 Peter 1:6, 7

Worthless
Matthew 10:29-31
Romans 8:14-16

Weak
Hebrews 13:5b, 6
Isaiah 40:28-31

Purposeless
Acts 17:26, 27
Ephesians 2:10

Try these practical suggestions from the same group of pastors' wives if you find yourself constantly grumbling, complaining, or finding fault:

1. Sing aloud the Scripture song, "This Is the Day That the Lord Has Made; Rejoice and Be Glad" (Psalm 118:24).
2. Read the book of Proverbs and take it seriously.
3. Try purposely substituting gratitude for complaining. Get a paper and pencil to make a list of blessings. Giving thanks can raise spirits as nothing else can.
4. Set aside a block of several days when you make up your mind with firmness not to be critical or complain. Make it a point not to fuss about small things or make mountains out of molehills. Mark the days on the calendar, and each evening, check to see how you are doing.
5. Remind yourself that on blue or tired-out days, other people's faults (especially your mate's) are glaring, sometimes irritating to the point of tears. On good days, other people's faults do not daunt us. After all, they belong to someone else.
6. To avoid boredom and self-pity that often accompany mundane household tasks, memorize these:
   1 Corinthians 10:31
   Matthew 20:26-28
   Romans 12:9-21

7. Too many demands on a woman's time can make her cross. A change of scenery, new activities, or planned time for yourself can renew and restore, often making fatigue and irritability disappear. Budget money for personal recreation. Plan into every day some time for hobbies and other things you thoroughly enjoy, such as reading, crocheting, bridge, sewing, baking, refinishing furniture, watching TV, etc. Say to yourself, "God loves me when I am relaxing, too."

8. For self-preservation, get up early. Use the uninterrupted time just for you. Enjoy the solitude of silence; listen to the friendly sound of a clock ticking; meditate on God; read the Bible; do a correspondence course. (One woman completed a prize-winning 6 x 9 foot hooked rug between the hours of 5:30 and 7:00 A.M. every morning.)

9. Make a list of things you have always wanted to accomplish. Choose one at a time and go for it . . . a college degree, a new hobby, writing poetry, tatting, learning French, etc. Reaching goals makes people happy. Doing new things adds freshness to life and makes you a more interesting companion.

10. Bless the one who hurts you. Instead of retaliating when someone has made you suffer, by pure willpower, actually pray God's blessing on that very one. How distinctive to give a blessing when everybody else in the world seems to be paying back evil for evil! (One woman commented: "I was constantly

complaining about Jim and the kids throwing their clothes around and messing up the house in general. I knew that a woman beautiful to God does not hold a grudge or blame others for her attitude. Following God's orders in Romans 12:14-21, I prayed for money for a new suit for Jim and that God would bless him with a more satisfying job and a new car because the old one was undependable in getting him to work. I asked for a more understanding teacher for one of the twins and new friends for our shy daughter when we moved. We never did get the new car, but I felt beautiful inside and pleased with myself as a wife and mother. I am trusting God to change their bad habits.")

11. Post this thought from Charles Spurgeon on the cupboard door: *Love stands in the presence of a fault with a finger on its lip.*

12. Ask your husband to pray with you about things that need changing in your life. He will appreciate your efforts to correct your own faults. Prayer can calm spirits and change feelings about each other. (One pastor says, "Couples accustomed to kneeling together before God seldom need my help for marriage problems.")

13. Instead of constantly commiserating with yourself, your husband, or your children, learn to communicate with God about problems. *The Living Bible* (2 Chronicles 16:9) says that God's eyes are searching back

and forth across the whole earth looking for righteous people so he can show his great power in helping them get out of trouble.

♥ ♥ ♥

Powerful mind menders from six women happily married a total of two hundred years:

"My own behavior, not my husband's, is all that I am responsible for before God."

"Anyone can make demands. It takes a strong person to spend time satisfying another person's needs."

"I am a daughter of the King." (See Ephesians 1:4, 5.)

"If I am sullen and grouchy at home, but gracious and friendly at church, work, and the garden club, there is something wrong in my life and I need to ask God to show me how to correct it."

"I must not allow my good attitude to depend on something or somebody. It is ridiculous for a born-again woman to allow her happiness to depend on such erratic things as how a three-year-old behaves today; whether or not a husband is cranky or friendly; or if there is enough money to pay every bill. My attitude should be dependent only on a continuing, stable relationship with God who loves me and provides for me at all times, night and day, no matter what."

"I cannot excuse my bad nature or habits by telling others 'That is just the way I am:' There is no place in the Bible that condones crabbiness, persistent hostility, stubborness, nasty tempers, impatience, unkindness, negativeness, quarrelsomeness, or lack of self-control, no matter how they were acquired or how deprived my childhood was."

♥ ♥ ♥

Test yourself. A domineering woman, especially one who grabs the upper hand under the guise of being helpful, is not beautiful. Often even quiet women have underhanded ways they themselves do not recognize as efforts to be boss. Take this mini Power Grab Test developed by an Atlanta marriage counselor who has written a book of advice for wives. A score of three or more "yesses" indicates you may have a heavy hand in your house.

1. Do I consistently tell my husband which route to take when driving because it is shorter or more scenic? (This kind of woman rides with a map in her hand.)
2. Do I assume he cannot handle his own affairs by making little interfering suggestions about his man-oriented personal business, work, club, or church affairs? Example: "Have you picked up the meat from the butcher as you said you would for the men's supper at church tonight?"

3. When questions are asked of both of us, do I almost always answer immediately myself, without deferring to him with a pause?
4. Do I often correct my husband in front of others?
5. Do I constantly begin my conversation with a demand for action or a question? (Questions demand answers.)
6. Do I often put down his ideas, even if sweetly, in favor of mine with, "Yes, but . . ." or "I have a better idea . . ." instead of saying "OK"?

Beautiful Outside: Helps and Hints
(from wives attending a Georgia Christian Family seminar)

Ask your husband how he wants you to look . . . your hair, your clothes, your makeup. Then, as much as you can, try to please him. (One wife says, "If he likes print dresses and you think they make your hips look big, at least try one. If he likes blonde hair, consider bleaching. If he favors Tigress perfume, wear it often even though it is not your favorite. That is what love in action is all about.")

♥ ♥ ♥

Attend a good grooming workshop for some new ideas, or go to a place where cosmetics are sold and ask for a free demonstration to learn how to expertly apply makeup yourself.

Do body care in private. As much as possible, cut toenails, put on cold cream, shave body hair, douche, or gargle behind closed doors. Let him see you when you are manicured and beautiful.

♥ ♥ ♥

Put a trip to the hairdresser into your regular budget. Remind yourself that beautifully styled hair is attractive to a man; a ponytail is not very alluring.

♥ ♥ ♥

Buy a hairdryer or a curling iron or electric rollers. Wearing curlers to bed is thoughtless and not very conducive to good sex.

♥ ♥ ♥

Try to look your best when your husband is at home. Looking great across the supper table from each other never hurts any marriage. Being neat and pretty around the house or to go shopping says to the family, "I love you enough to look nice so you can be proud of me."

♥ ♥ ♥

Purchase a good makeup mirror with magnifying glass. Use it often for close-up inspection and to apply cosmetics.

Determine to keep your shape shapely. Buy a full-length mirror to study yourself. Use bathroom scales. Do you need a diet? To help lose weight, one woman who dieted eighty pounds away suggests: stop snacking; ask yourself why you are eating right now; tape a picture of a woman with a beautiful figure you admire on the refrigerator door; hang a too-small garment you would love to wear near the refrigerator; eat meals slower; stay away from the grocery store when you are hungry; absolutely refuse to keep ice cream, candy, and baked goods in the house.

Never, never kiss him if your lipstick is not blotted!

UNCOMMON
COMMUNICATION
7

After a spat, what Hostile Harry can fail to get the
"I love you" message from a wife who hangs a
banner in the bedroom saying: *I will be swift to
hear, slow to speak, slow to wrath, as the Bible
suggests in James 1:19?* What Quiet Quentin can
remain silent and noncommunicative about his
feelings when his wife expresses her longings by
playing the haunting song "Do You Love Me?"
from *Fiddler on the Roof?* This is creative communication, yet who thinks of it? It not only
makes a marriage sparkle with distinctiveness, but
keeps the friendship factor intact while getting
the message across.

Some wives express a need for tactful ideas that
will warm a heart, sponsor a smile, or tickle a rib
to get their mate's attention and communicate
love in unique ways. Others say they need attitude

adjusters that will change their own frame of mind and thus minister to a husband's hurting spirit or bitter temperament, making him more receptive to open and honest conversation.

Many thick books have been written about couples' communication, but advice is often general as well as generous, lacking practical and simple tips and pointers. Yet, walls can sometimes be broken down and the old glow revived with a little practical living room therapy. Here are helps and hints to improve your own communication and help you live more easily with a mate who may not yet have learned to communicate very well with you.

Ideas That Are Uncommon Communicators

Paste together letters and pictures from magazines to make up a message. Post it by the door, on his dresser, desk, or perhaps send it to him at work. (One clever wife told her husband she was pregnant this fun way.)

♥ ♥ ♥

Run a small ad in the classified section of the local paper on Father's Day, his birthday, or your anniversary. Cost will be minimal. Here are samples written by three Alabama women:

Daddies may come and daddies may go,
But you are the best daddy I know. Love, Sue.

Leslie, *Je t'adore.* You are the greatest. Birthday love from Marion. (Both studied French together in high school.)

Breaker, Breaker, how about your Big Blue Eyes come-on? I love you more than yesterday, less than tomorrow. 10-4? Signed. "Pet." (From a pair of CB enthusiasts.)

♥ ♥ ♥

Spell a special short message in large letters on big white discs cut from construction paper, one letter per disc. Mail them to him mixed up in a box, to be assembled like a puzzle. (Fran's husband was four hundred miles away for three months working on a construction project. Her disc message was: *I'm flying to Toledo. Meet me at the Holiday Inn at six on Friday and we will celebrate your birthday all weekend.*)

♥ ♥ ♥

If you have both been too busy, write with your finger on a fogged window or mirror: *Spending time together communicates "I love you." Let's. I do.*

♥ ♥ ♥

Read aloud to him Elizabeth Barrett Browning's poem that begins, "How do I love thee? Let me count the ways. . . ."

Write a love letter marked "personal" and mail it to his office. (Jan wondered why Artie did not say a word about her carefully worded letter written on fancy stationery. On vacation the following week, Artie commented, "My best girl friend sent me a racy letter at the office last Friday. What do you think I should do about it?")

♥ ♥ ♥

Pin an *I love you* note on his pillow if you are going out alone in the evening and do not expect to return until after his bedtime.

♥ ♥ ♥

Put a note in his golf glove, hunting gear, or fishing tackle saying, "Hurry home. I am waiting for you."

♥ ♥ ♥

Hold his arm while walking down the street. Touch him as he walks by in the hall or kitchen. Touching says, "I love you."

♥ ♥ ♥

Lessons in Better Communication from Wives and Other Experts

From Angie:
  It is sometimes easier to share thoughts with Phil when we are doing dishes or taking a walk together than when we sit down and have a talk.

From Liza:

My husband, Tim, is very quiet. It hurts me
when he just doesn't talk much to me and I find
myself repaying him by purposely withholding
bits of news from him or not answering his
questions completely. I know he cares deeply
for me even if he has never learned to show it
very well, but there is a barrier between us. It
helps to look for the many ways he *does* communicate his love and to allow him freedom to do
it his own way . . . touching, gifts, doing small
things around the house, helping with the kids,
staying home and loving it, etc.

From Teresa:

My listening is an act of love. Lately I have
learned to look my man in the eye when he
talks to me, because he says it is devastating to
say important things to me when my eyes are
not meeting his. I try to think to myself, "He
needs a confidante, so I need to listen closely.
He has chosen me out of all his other friends to
share with."

From Dee:

I try to be the kind of listener that God is. He
allows unlimited access, with open eyes and
ears, day and night, every day of every year.

From Ellie:

I think that God, in trying to communicate his
will to me, often speaks through others who are

in my life, especially when I am making decisions. That makes it doubly important to listen well and be open to what my mate has to say.

From Julie:
Beating around the bush makes my husband angry. When I want something, telling him exactly what is on my mind usually works best:

"I am tired out. I would like a weekend at Jekyll Island all by myself, no kids, no phones, no interruptions. Do you think we could arrange that?"

"I need thirty dollars for throw rugs in the bedroom."

My fifteen-year-old daughter showed me how well this direct approach works when she met her weary father entering the front door after work and said to him, "Will you drive me into the city to get a silver Bach trumpet mouthpiece for the school band concert tonight?" Away they went in rush-hour traffic to get her heart's desire.

♥ ♥ ♥

From Nell:
After months of therapy with a Christian psychologist, I finally could admit that a secluded person like myself, who withdraws from others, might be self-centered and even lazy. My therapist showed me that communication is work and interaction tiring. It takes much effort to listen closely and then activate the brain to

think through an intelligent and appropriate response. The Bible never condones a life style of isolation or laziness.

From Ardis:
Noncommunicative people seem indifferent and stingy about giving themselves away. Indifference (not caring) is the opposite of love and is always a put-down of the other.

From Alice:
For years, Bert would say to me, "I don't like being around you when you are angry." My resentful response would always be, "But, I'm not angry." I was brought up in a family that hid feelings, especially adverse ones. It took a whole year of counseling with my wise pastor before I realized I had been programmed to ignore my feelings for so long that I was actually unaware they were there. I now know I don't need to be ashamed of my feelings and that my union with Bert is enhanced by sharing them, whatever they may be. Hiding feelings involves pride and self-centeredness, hurts those around me, and makes me feel lonely because I am not getting close to anyone. Tuning into my own thoughts and feelings took practice. My pastor suggested I spend quiet time daily focusing on my feelings and writing them down, first about one person, then another, then about issues.

From Tina, who is doing a college research paper on communication:

Only about 3 percent of communication comes through words. I found that studies show nearly 58 percent of what we communicate to others is through facial expressions and about 40 percent through voice inflection or gestures. That reminded me that smirks, sighs, scowls, and giggles, as well as broad friendly smiles, let my partner know how I feel.

From Beth:

Playing the martyr or giving the silent treatment cuts off communication and is probably sin. My silence infuriates Jack and causes confusion because he has to guess what I am thinking. I have come to realize that my silence is often an attempt to control him by refusing to reveal where I stand on issues.

From Betty:

Communicating legitimate complaints with a touch of humor helps:

"You talc too much."

"You are afflicted with a deadly case of Monday morning mattressitis."

"Sitty Slickers get heart trouble. Let's get out and play more tennis."

From Betty's pastor-counselor husband:

Some people never talk above the superficial level . . . the weather, kids . . . in short, about things. But good and satisfying communication that provides closeness for a couple allows the other to look inside you and see what is going on there. Noncommunicators feel uncomfortable continuing a conversation when it gets too close to revealing feelings and they have subtle ways to cut it off, inadvertently hurting the partner badly. Below are ways commonly used to destroy perfectly good conversations that become threatening. Check yourself to see how you are doing.

Inattentiveness. While Jim tells Ann about his new flower garden, Ann eyes her fingernails and then flips to a new TV channel.

Interrupting. Jim shares with Ann the results of last night's bridge game. When he gets to the punch line, Ann sees the dog chasing a car and interrupts by shouting, "Spotty, stop that right now! Get back here!"

Being judgmental. Jim tells Ann his disappointment about not getting a promotion at the plant. He feels relieved to talk about it until Ann says, "If only you had stayed later at work on Mondays and taken that trip to Chicago, you would have been promoted. You never do the little extras Mr. Patton suggests."

Turning a good conversation into an argument.

Jim: It was a great party, Hon. The hors d'oeuvres were the best ever and we invited just the

right crowd. Your white dress showed off
your tan and you were a knockout. . . .

Ann: I hate that dress. You are always telling me
how good I look and I think you just want
something to say. You know I need a new
dress, but we never seem to have the money.

**Answering a question with another question
instead of giving a reply.**

Jim: I was thinking today how much more I love
you now than before.

Ann: Before what?

**Answering with a trite remark or a cliché
(which is really someone else's words and
thus safe, allowing isolation to remain).**

Jim: Do you think we can get the mortgage to
buy our new house?

Ann: Sure. Sure. Just bring an honest face.

**Giving advice when your partner only wants
a listening ear.**

Jim: My back has been aching again lately. It gives
me a lot of trouble at night.

Ann: You should get a new chair for your office
and quit tennis.

**Changing the subject abruptly because of
embarrassment.**

Ann (feeling flattered): The new guy at work
really gave me the eye all last week. He
didn't believe I was married until I refused a
date for the third time today.

Jim (not willing to reveal his jealousy): Yeah? Did you hear about the accident down on Elm Street this morning? Six people were hurt.

Not answering at all or making short, unrevealing responses.

"Yup."

"Nope."

"I guess so."

"I'm going now. Be back later."

Pretending you do not have any opinions or feelings.

Jim: Do you want to go to the meeting tonight?

Ann: I don't care.

or

Jim: How do you feel now that you have actually put in your application for the new job?

Ann: Oh, all right, I guess.

or

Jim: What did you think of the Republican Convention on TV today?

Ann: I don't remember what went on. (She walks away.)

Speaking with a snarling voice (often an unrecognized habit except to others). This is a sure-fire way to drive your partner off. Who, after all, wants to continue talking with someone who seems angry?

Making inappropriate body gestures that bespeak noncaring or making fun. This includes such actions as: shrugging shoulders, nodding for yes or no answers, turning your back, slouching in the chair, mocking by mimicking a favorite dialect, or making funny faces for a laugh while giving an answer.

This same pastor-counselor suggests improving communication by enrolling in the Minnesota Couples' Communication seminar in your area. For a list of instructors, write:

International Communications Programs
300 Clifton Avenue, The Carriage House
Minneapolis, Minnesota 55403

He also suggests these books:
Getting to Know You by Marjorie Umphrey (Harvest Books)
How to Live with Your Feelings by Philip J. Swihart (InterVarsity Press)
Why Am I Afraid to Tell You Who I Am? by John Powell (Argus)
The Secret of Staying in Love by John Powell (Argus)
Communication: Key to Marriage by H. Norman Wright (Regal Books)
When You Don't Agree by James Fairfield (Herald Press)
After You've Said I Do by Dwight H. and Fleming H. Small (Revell)

♥ ♥ ♥

WHEN HE TRAVELS
8

Joan (with hands on hips): I'm glad you are
       finally home. Jimmy needs a spanking. The
       washer broke down and I need you to help
       me take the dog to the vet for his shot.

Mark: You just don't know how tired I am. There
       are two stopovers on that flight from
       California. For heaven's sake, leave me
       alone for a while, will you?

Joan clobbered Mark with demands and complaints as soon as he entered the front door from
his business trip. She could have saved gloomy-day
descriptions until a time when he was better able
to cope, perhaps after a hearty meal or the following day. Her first words could have been a balm to
heal the wounds received in his day's work:

"I realize how much I miss you when you are
away for a while."

"You look hot and tired; I'll get you some iced tea."

"I am glad you are back."

With a little forethought, a wife can often make her husband's travels easier, and their home an appealing place that his mind returns to over and over when he is hundreds of miles away. Ideas from six salesmen's wives:

While he is packing and getting ready to leave, ask, "Can I do anything for you while you are gone?" He will probably be miles behind in everything after a few days away. (One wife polished all her husband's shoes. Another weeded his garden.)

♥ ♥ ♥

Pack a bag of cookies in his suitcase. It will save him putting his clothes back on to go down to the motel lobby for a late snack.

♥ ♥ ♥

Hide a note in his underwear for the third or fourth day saying:

> On the day you read this, I will be asking my boss for a raise. Please pray for me.
> I always miss you in bed at night beside me.
> I will have a surprise for you when you get home. You will like it.
> I love you. You are my world.

Make a list of family addresses, phone numbers, and birthdays for him to carry when he travels.

♥ ♥ ♥

Hide a little photo of you or the family in his suitcase.

♥ ♥ ♥

Be positive and excited about his trip before he leaves and the children probably will be, too.

♥ ♥ ♥

Know the details of his trip activities so that you and the kids can follow him along on a map or schedule and discuss what he is doing on a given day.

♥ ♥ ♥

Help the kids keep a diary of daily doings at home to share with Dad when he returns. Have them cut pictures from old magazines to illustrate and add a couple of pages a day. (Says a Georgia mother of four, "With all the hustle and hassle of a big family, I never would otherwise have remembered to share with him the funny antics, such as when the baby spit out a ping pong ball so Grandma could feed him mashed banana, or the way our gun-shy collie ran under the bed when she heard us cracking nuts for the Christmas fruit cakes.")

Keep busy and happy at home while he is gone. Catch up on housework, wallpaper a room, straighten drawers and closets, take an adult study course, invite friends in. Or, conversely, leave housework and spend the time for fun projects such as sewing, reading, or a hobby that you have not had time for lately.

♥ ♥ ♥

Call him long distance just before breakfast to say good morning. Keep in mind the time difference.

♥ ♥ ♥

Call him at the motel some evening and say, "I just wanted to tell you I miss you right now and wish you were here."

♥ ♥ ♥

On a day that will be difficult for him, send a telegram to his motel, or a carnation boutonniere with card saying, "We are thinking about you."

♥ ♥ ♥

If his stay is lengthy, type out "You are looking at the man I love" and tape it on a small mirror to send him. (One woman wrote this on her husband's bathroom mirror with lipstick when he returned home. He later added "wo," changing "man" to "woman." An army wife, whose husband was on a month's temporary duty away from

home, sent him a handmade 18″ red heart pillow
on Valentine's Day. An attached button said, "Want
to pet?")

♥ ♥ ♥

When he returns:

Teach the kids the "When Daddy gets home"
routine . . . no questions, no complaints, no
requests until he has had time to change his
clothes, putter, and relax.

♥ ♥ ♥

Meet him by the car, put your arm around his
waist, and walk him to the house. Say, "I couldn't
wait until you got home."

♥ ♥ ♥

Take the whole family to meet him at the
airport, all dressed up in their Sunday best.

♥ ♥ ♥

Once in a while, go alone to pick up your man
at the airport. Meet him at the gate. Wear his
favorite dress and look beautiful. Let the kids
know it is a special time for both of you.

♥ ♥ ♥

Have his favorite music playing when he comes
in the house.

Hang a "Welcome Home" banner by the front door and sing "Happy Homecoming to You" to the tune of "Happy Birthday."

♥ ♥ ♥

Tie a huge yellow ribbon on the old oak (or peach or whatever) tree to greet him as in the song.

♥ ♥ ♥

Sometimes, unpack his suitcase.

♥ ♥ ♥

Plan a family time to hear about his trip and to share news with him. Set a special hour such as when the clock strikes seven or right after Daddy comes out of the shower.

♥ ♥ ♥

HOW TO LOVE
YOUR MAN
CREATIVELY

EVEN THOUGH
YOU GET ANGRY
9

She is a night person. He goes to bed at ten.

She is always late. He learned punctuality in the army.

She is shy, a homebody. He loves people and parties.

How do two vastly different people with diverse backgrounds, values, and ideas function as one even to settle simple questions such as where to spend Thanksgiving, how much spending money each gets, who puts the kids to bed, which movie to attend? Solutions to more explosive questions such as whether an in-law will come to live with the family, which car to buy, or whether the wife gives up her good job to move for the sake of her husband's promotion are difficult.

Differences of opinion are natural. Arguments are inevitable. In a way, they are a healthy sign, an indication that the marriage is intact and the partners have not lost interest. But agreeable disagreement must be learned and a couple needs to find ways to argue constructively, to make up creatively, and to live tolerantly with things that cannot be changed.

Effective confrontation. Cheryl feels resentful, burdened with a full-time job and the complete housework load. She needs to talk it out with Frank. Cheryl has tried before to confront him, but once Frank continued reading his *Tennis* magazine and another time he walked away to tell their five-year-old to stay off the new lawn. This time she has a better plan:

"Frank, I have something important to talk over with you. Let's meet in the den at eight o'clock after I put the kids to bed."

Frank is pleased with Cheryl's straightforward-ness, and a little surprised that she made an appointment with her own husband. He is curious about the subject of their talk. Cheryl thinks he will be paying close attention this time because she let him know how important it is to her by going out of the way to get them together. There will be no interruptions. She purposely postponed the discussion until she could spend time coming to grips with her own feelings and thinking through what they are before she speaks with him. Her aim is not to put Frank down, but to let him know how she feels and to ask for help. Over and over she uses the words "I feel. . . ."

"I feel frustrated and angry because I have not been able to share this very well with you before."

"I feel tired out. . . ."

"I feel hurt that you did not seem to understand. . . ."

"I feel all alone with this problem. . . ."

Cheryl has learned to confront effectively. She is sharing her heart, not her ammunition. She has attacked the problem, not her mate.

Making up creatively. Another time, Cheryl and Frank argue about money. After a few days, the kids are beginning to notice Mom's and Dad's scowls and are hurt by their parents' silence around the house. They wonder if it is their fault. How do you make up and keep sensitive egos intact?

Cheryl makes *"I Love You, Anyway"* badges, pins one on herself, and tapes others to the evening paper, Frank's tie rack, his toolbox, and the shower handle. It is a signal that she is willing to make up. Frank reacts by making his own badge that says: *Frank loves Cheryl even when they argue; let's all go over to the Dairy Queen.* Cheryl is pleased. She responds with a smile and a private note stuffed in his shirt pocket that says, "Later, we could even continue making up after dark."

Frank was softened by Cheryl's thoughtful, loving, and unique approach. Cheryl has learned to make up creatively.

Your attitude toward the unchangeable. An Alabama wife who had been pondering divorce and a new husband says: "The turning point came when a friend reminded me that there is only one kind of man to marry—a sinner—and that if I remarried I would have to adjust to some new sinner's set of faults. It helps to remember that a man has only one kind of woman to marry, too."

The wife of a Christian psychologist states: "The arguments got fewer when I realized that my husband was not making me angry as I had told him over and over, but that he was just bringing out of me all the resentment, self-pity, and selfishness I had built into myself over the years."

From a pastor's wife who admitted constant criticism of her husband and almost daily quarrels: "After lengthy prayer beseeching God to stop our arguing because I knew divorce would dishonor his name, God showed me that he is the author of my husband's personality and that what I view as faults are really a tool God uses to make me cling to him for solutions. When I began to admit that only God is powerful and authoritative enough to bring about such change, I was able to purposely pass over the irritating qualities and trust God, through my prayers, to make alterations in my husband if they were needed."

♥ ♥ ♥

Here are favorite marriage menders from a group of Georgia wives that will help you live easier when you are angry at your wonderful sinner:

After an argument, ask God to show you the positive side of your man. List all his good qualities. Then put the list in your wallet and go over it every time you get irritated with him.

♥ ♥ ♥

Practice the presence of God. Picture him guarding and regarding your marriage at all times.

♥ ♥ ♥

Do not walk out in the middle of an argument.

♥ ♥ ♥

If you think you are going to have a crying spell, go some place alone and get it out of your system. Then come back and say, "I have unloaded the hysterics and now I can tell you how I feel."

♥ ♥ ♥

Determine not to let your husband's naturally harsher personality hurt your feelings. Do not hold it against him. Men are just gruffer than women.

♥ ♥ ♥

Remind yourself that face-to-face confrontation is not sin, but that stubborn silence and refusing to talk things out can be. Someone has said that silence is not golden, but cowardly. Honestly expressing feelings can clear the air and open the way to solutions. One husband comments, "I really would not respect a mealy-mouthed wife who agrees with me all the time. I would feel cheated if she did not share her differences of opinion with me, especially when I am making hard decisions or there is some vague wall between us."

♥ ♥ ♥

Books to help settle conflicts effectively with love:

The Love-Fight by David Augsburger (Herald Press)

When You Don't Agree by James G. T. Fairfield (Herald Press)

♥ ♥ ♥

If you are not born-again Christians, take God into your marriage. You can ask a pastor how. After committing her life to Christ three years ago, Jane says, "When God entered our lives, a higher authority began to be our advisor, and now instead of each demanding our own way, we often ask, 'Lord, what do *you* want us to do in this situation?'"

♥ ♥ ♥

Ask God to help you accept the things you cannot change.

Settle arguments before the sun goes down, as the Bible recommends in Ephesians 4:26.

♥ ♥ ♥

Speak softly as much as you can during an argument. Tell your mate how you feel without shouting. Arguments can be settled just as well with reasonable voice levels, and a suddenly lower voice volume will catch him off guard, pleasantly. "A soft answer turneth away wrath" (Proverbs 15:1).

♥ ♥ ♥

Say to your partner during an argument:
"I will try to understand how you feel about this matter."
"This much I know. You are a good man and you deserve a good wife who understands."
"Let's write down the points of agreement we have and go from there."

♥ ♥ ♥

Say to yourself:
"I do not need to be right all the time."
"It requires maturity to accept criticism graciously."
"My partner may not be trying to hurt me. He is just seeing things in a different way. Differences of opinion do not make one of us right, the other wrong. They are not marks of inferiority."
"When I am angry I will never be more vulnera-

ble to the temptations of hatred, resentment, or even violence. My anger needs self-control as a partner."

♥ ♥ ♥

Determine to keep hurtful words and troublesome phrases out of the discussion when you are angry. Avoid:

"I told you so."
"You are just like your mother (or father)."
"George, why is it you always . . . ?" (Phrases such as "You always . . ." or "You never . . ." do not help settle an argument.)

♥ ♥ ♥

Never, never say to your husband, "You should not feel that way." His feelings are uniquely his own and he *does* feel that way. Try to understand and empathize. Asking him to tell you why he feels the way he does or simply saying, "I understand" will keep the conversation rolling.

♥ ♥ ♥

When you are hurt or angry, purposely force your mind to recall three happy times you shared together previously, such as making love at a vacation spot or in a particular hotel room, holding each other to make up after an earlier argument, or his first joyous day home after a serious illness at the hospital. Remind yourself that every marriage has its good and bad times and that good times will come again.

When you are ready to make up, but he is still silent, type this on a card and stick it up somewhere:

   Love is: Trying not to give the silent treatment for too long.

♥ ♥ ♥

You can begin the make-up process after a fight by printing the letters PBPGINFWMY on a sheet of paper and pinning it to your lapel. When he asks what it means, tell him the letters stand for: *Please be patient: God is not finished with me yet.*

♥ ♥ ♥

After an argument, put your hand on his arm or shoulder and say nothing. Touching shows caring, no demands attached.

♥ ♥ ♥

Forget ancient history. Determine not to stockpile his negative attitudes and bad deeds in your memory to be dredged up during future arguments.

♥ ♥ ♥

After a fight, try to forget by purposely getting busy. Clear out the garage; mop the kitchen floor; walk the dog; clean the attic; or go to the library for a good book.

Some people bury the hatchet but never forget where. If you find it hard to forgive, remind yourself that it takes a lot of energy to hold a grudge and that there is great freedom in forgiveness. A grudge enslaves your mind to one subject for days.

♥ ♥ ♥

Remind yourself that pride is a cold bed partner, and that being constantly irritated is a great way to wipe out good sex.

♥ ♥ ♥

Good words with which to make up after an argument:
"I was a witch this morning and I apologize."
"Honey, I haven't been very loving."
"You may be right."
"We can still continue to love each other even though we are not entirely satisfied with things around here."
"When you love someone, you want God's best for him. I want God's best for you."
"Even though this one thing bothers us, I still love you in a lot of other ways."

♥ ♥ ♥

A good motto: "If I am wrong, I will say so. If I am right I will shut up."

Say the words "I am sorry" when you are wrong.
Serving his favorite dessert to make up is just not
as good.

♥ ♥ ♥

Suggest that you pray together after a fight. It is
hard to hold bad feelings about someone you pray
with.

♥ ♥ ♥

Other Living Books Best-sellers

LORD, YOU LOVE TO SAY YES by Ruth Harms Calkin. In this collection of prayer-poems the author speaks openly and honestly with her Lord about hopes and dreams, longings and frustrations, and her observations of life. 07-3824 $2.95.

MORE THAN A CARPENTER by Josh McDowell. A hard-hitting book for people who are skeptical about Jesus' deity, his resurrection, and his claims on their lives. 07-4552 $2.95.

NOW IS YOUR TIME TO WIN by Dave Dean. In this true-life story, Dean shares how he locked into seven principles that enabled him to bounce back from failure to success. Read about successful men and women—from sports and entertainment celebrities to the ordinary people next door—and discover how you too can bounce back from failure to success! 07-4727 $2.95.

THE POSITIVE POWER OF JESUS CHRIST by Norman Vincent Peale. All his life the author has been leading men and women to Jesus Christ. In this book he tells of his boyhood encounters with Jesus and of his spiritual growth as he attended seminary and began his world-renowned ministry. 07-4914 $3.95.

REASONS by Josh McDowell and Don Stewart. In a convenient question-and-answer format, the authors address many of the commonly asked questions about the Bible and evolution. 07-5287 $3.95.

ROCK by Bob Larson. A well-researched and penetrating look at today's rock music and rock performers, their lyrics, and their lifestyles. 07-5686 $3.50.

SHAPE UP FROM THE INSIDE OUT by John R. Throop. Learn how to conquer the problem of being overweight! In this honest, often humorous book, Throop shares his own personal struggle with this area and how he gained fresh insight about the biblical relationship between physical and spiritual fitness. 07-5899 $2.95.

TAKE ME HOME by Bonnie Jamison. This touching, candid story of the author's relationship with her dying mother will offer hope and assurance to those dealing with an aging parent, relative, or friend. 07-6901 $3.50.

TELL ME AGAIN, LORD, I FORGET by Ruth Harms Calkin. You will easily identify with Calkin in this collection of prayer-poems about the challenges, peaks, and quiet moments of each day. 07-6990 $3.50.

THROUGH GATES OF SPLENDOR by Elisabeth Elliot. This unforgettable story of five men who braved the Auca Indians has become one of the most famous missionary books of all times. 07-7151 $3.95.

WAY BACK IN THE HILLS by James C. Hefley. The story of Hefley's colorful childhood in the Ozarks makes reflective reading for those who like a nostalgic journey into the past. 07-7821 $3.95.

Other Living Books Best-sellers

THE ANGEL OF HIS PRESENCE by Grace Livingston Hill. This book captures the romance of John Wentworth Stanley and a beautiful young woman whose influence causes John to reevaluate his well-laid plans for the future. 07-0047 $2.50.

HOW TO BE HAPPY THOUGH MARRIED by Tim LaHaye. One of America's most successful marriage counselors gives practical, proven advice for marital happiness. 07-1499 $3.50.

JOHN, SON OF THUNDER by Ellen Gunderson Traylor. In this saga of adventure, romance, and discovery, travel with John—the disciple whom Jesus loved—down desert paths, through the courts of the Holy City, to the foot of the cross. Journey with him from his luxury as a privileged son of Israel to the bitter hardship of his exile on Patmos. 07-1903 $4.95.

KAREN'S CHOICE by Janice Hermansen. College students Karen and Jon fall in love and are heading toward marriage when Karen discovers she is pregnant. Struggle with Karen and Jon through the choices they make and observe how they cope with the consequences and eventually find the forgiveness of Christ. 07-2027 $3.50.

LIFE IS TREMENDOUS! by Charlie "Tremendous" Jones. Believing that enthusiasm makes the difference, Jones shows how anyone can be happy, involved, relevant, productive, healthy, and secure in the midst of a high-pressure, commercialized society. 07-2184 $2.50.

LOOKING FOR LOVE IN ALL THE WRONG PLACES by Joe White. Using wisdom gained from many talks with young people, White steers teens in the right direction to find love and fulfillment in a personal relationship with God. 07-3825 $3.50.

LORD, I KEEP RUNNING BACK TO YOU by Ruth Harms Calkin. In prayer-poems tinged with wonder, joy, humanness, and questioning, the author speaks for all of us who are groping and learning together what it means to be God's child. 07-3819 $3.50.

SUCCESS: THE GLENN BLAND METHOD by Glenn Bland. The author shows how to set goals and make plans that really work. His ingredients of success include spiritual, financial, educational, and recreational balances. 07-6689 $3.50.

MOUNTAINS OF SPICES by Hannah Hurnard. Here is an allegory comparing the nine spices mentioned in the Song of Solomon to the nine fruits of the Spirit. A story of the glory of surrender by the author of *HINDS' FEET ON HIGH PLACES.* 07-4611 $3.50.

THE NEW MOTHER'S BOOK OF BABY CARE by Marjorie Palmer and Ethel Bowman. From what you will need to clothe the baby to how to know when to call the doctor, this book will give you all the basic knowledge necessary to be the parent your child needs. 07-4695 $2.95.

Other Living Books Best-sellers

ANSWERS by Josh McDowell and Don Stewart. In a question-and-answer format, the authors tackle sixty-five of the most-asked questions about the Bible, God, Jesus Christ, miracles, other religions, and creation. 07-0021 $3.95.

THE BEST CHRISTMAS PAGEANT EVER by Barbara Robinson. A delightfully wild and funny story about what happens to a Christmas program when the "Horrible Herdman" brothers and sisters are miscast in the roles of the biblical Christmas story characters. 07-0137 $2.50.

BUILDING YOUR SELF-IMAGE by Josh McDowell. Here are practical answers to help you overcome your fears, anxieties, and lack of self-confidence. Learn how God's higher image of who you are can take root in your heart and mind. 07-1395 $3.95.

THE CHILD WITHIN by Mari Hanes. The author shares insights she gained from God's Word during her own pregnancy. She identifies areas of stress, offers concrete data about the birth process, and points to God's sure promises that he will "gently lead those that are with young." 07-0219 $2.95.

400 WAYS TO SAY I LOVE YOU by Alice Chapin. Perhaps the flame of love has almost died in your marriage. Maybe you have a good marriage that just needs a little "spark." Here is a book especially for the woman who wants to rekindle the flame of romance in her marriage; who wants creative, practical, useful ideas to show the man in her life that she cares. 07-0919 $2.50.

GIVERS, TAKERS, AND OTHER KINDS OF LOVERS by Josh McDowell and Paul Lewis. This book bypasses vague generalities about love and sex and gets right to the basic questions: Whatever happened to sexual freedom? What's true love like? Do men respond differently than women? If you're looking for straight answers about God's plan for love and sexuality, this book was written for you. 07-1031 $2.95.

HINDS' FEET ON HIGH PLACES by Hannah Hurnard. A classic allegory of a journey toward faith that has sold more than a million copies! 07-1429 $3.95.

LORD, COULD YOU HURRY A LITTLE? by Ruth Harms Calkin. These prayer-poems from the heart of a godly woman trace the inner workings of the heart, following the rhythms of the day and the seasons of the year with expectation and love. 07-3816 $2.95.

WHAT WIVES WISH THEIR HUSBANDS KNEW ABOUT WOMEN by James Dobson. The best-selling author of *DARE TO DISCIPLINE* and *THE STRONG-WILLED CHILD* brings us this vital book that speaks to the unique emotional needs and aspirations of today's woman. An immensely practical, interesting guide. 07-7896 $3.50.

The books listed are available at your bookstore. If unavailable, send check with order to cover retail price plus $1.00 per book for postage and handling to:

Christian Book Service
Box 80
Wheaton, Illinois 60189

Prices and availability subject to change without notice. Allow 4–6 weeks for delivery.